Short Monologues for Auditions

Frank Catalano

Lexington Avenue Press
Copyright © 2013 Frank Catalano
All rights reserved.
ISBN: 148236980X
ISBN-13: 9781482369809

Short Monologues for Auditions

TABLE OF CONTENTS

Introduction 1

What is a monologue? 3

Why do I have to do monologue? 5

How do I select a monologue that's right for me? 6

Don't just rattle through a speech – treat
your monologue as it were a scene 7

What's the best way to memorize my lines and
create a physical life for my character? 9

Performing a monologue for an audition – How to create an
implementation strategy 10

Creating a performance dynamic - How to make a creative box to play in. 10

How to play each moment as if it were part of a larger mosaic 11

Using "What If?" 11

How to create the "moment before" 13

How to create "now" using specific beats 13

How to create the "moment after" 16

How to begin a monologue at an audition 17

Who should I look at when I perform an audition monologue? 19

How do I end my audition monologue? 19

How to have fun at an audition 21

THE MONOLOGUES

#1 CONFESSIONS OF A SERVER 24

#2 LAUNDRY 25

#3 RESCUE 26

#4 HOLD DOWN THE SEATS 27

#5 SITTING SOMEWHERE OUTSIDE 28

#6 THE CLEANSE 29

#7 SPIRIT 30

#8 CONFESSIONS OF A SERVER – *NEVER* ORDER FISH ON A SUNDAY 31

#9 CONFESSIONS OF A SERVER – THE BAD TIPPER 32

#10 THANK YOU 33

#11 WOMAN'S WORK – CLEANING (MALE) 34

#12 WOMAN'S WORK – CLEANING (FEMALE) 36

#13 DILLY DALLY 37

#14 STEPPING ON THE CRACKS 38

#15 EMPLOYEE AT WILL 39

#16 SANITY 40

#17 VIETNAM AND THE FORT HAMILTON LAMENT 41

#18 PALACE HOTEL - NEW YORK CITY 42

#19   I'M NOT HERE RIGHT NOW 43

#20   HOW DEEP TO DIG A HOLE 44

#21   LISTENING 45

#22   ARCHIPELEGO 46

#23   PENELOPE CRUISE 47

#24   SHE LOOKS GREAT IN THE DARK 48

#25   BAD HAIR DAY 49

#26   CRAZY ASS BEE 50

#27   DOG PEOPLE AND CAT PEOPLE 51

#28   LIVING INSIDE A HEFTY BAG 52

#29   VISUAL AUDITORY 53

#30   WASH YOUR HANDS 54

#31   ELMER FUDD PULLING THE TRAIN WHISTLE 55

#32   PAPER PLANES 56

#33   LITTLE WHITE LIES 57

#34   ELEPHANT DREAM 58

#35   ROAD KILL 59

#36   DEFRIENDED 60

#37   IF YOU WALK AWAY 61

#38   HAPPY FOR YOU 62

#	Title	Page
#39	TEXTING	63
#40	THE ESSAY	65
#41	THE TIARA (MALE)	66
#42	THE BABY BENCH	67
#43	CONTEMPLATION OF SELF	68
#44	TUESDAY	69
#45	MICKEY MOUSE T-SHIRT	70
#46	ELEMENTS OF STYLE	71
#47	DREAMING OF PARIS	72
#48	ROMANTIC	73
#49	LITTLE BLACK DRESS	74
#50	HEMLOCK	75
#51	THINGS PEOPLE SAY	76
#52	STATE OF GRACE	77
#53	DUMB WAYS TO DIE	78
#54	I ALWAYS REMIND PEOPLE OF OTHER PEOPLE	80
#55	AT LEAST YOU'RE NOT LYING	81
#56	EXHALE	82
#57	NOCTURNE	83
#58	LIKE BUTTER	84

#59 GOING HOME 85

#60 PLEASE DON'T TRY THIS AT HOME 86

#61 COOKING A POUND CAKE 87

#62 A TEMPORARY PET 88

#63 NECKTIE PARLOR 89

#64 MELANCHOLY 90

#65 THIS TIME 91

#66 DECONSTRUCTION 92

#67 ALWAYS 93

#68 IF I COULD ONLY BE THIN 94

#69 SHAMAN 95

#70 CRACKIN ROCKS 96

Introduction

As an author, I have written several monologue books including **ART OF THE MONOLGUE** and **WHITE KNIGHT BLACK NIGHT** – both of which focused on the performance of a monologue as an artistic work. This current volume focuses on the presentation of monologues specifically for the purpose of auditions and acting classes. The difference here is that the actual selection and presentation of the material is focused more upon the actor's abilities and type than the performance or the material. Why short monologues? As an acting teacher, I have always advised my students **"less is more."** What does that actually mean? In this case, I want the actor to focus specifically on a given purpose in the presentation of each piece. The given purpose of an audition is to provide the auditioner a sample of your acting abilities, your demeanor, your ability to take direction and ultimately to determine whether or not you are the right fit for what they are looking for. But, lets be honest, a casting director is rarely if ever going to have you perform a monologue if they are reading people for a specific role. They will just have you perform the actual lines of the character that you are reading for. So what would be the purpose of a monologue? In a larger sense, a director of a theatre company, a university theatre school, an agent or manager might want to see how you perform prepared material. They would want to see how you create the moment on your own so they can have an idea of the kind of actor you really are. To accomplish this, you need to present something that's brief, to the point and gives them an idea of who you are and what you can do. They don't need the whole performance, just a sample. An actor should have at least two short contemporary monologues (one comedy and one dramatic) ready to go at all times. If you want to be totally prepared you can add at least one or two short classical monologues to your acting arsenal. But here's the rub. If you prepare, well-known material from familiar sources, most auditioners will have seen and heard other actors do these same monologues. Here, you run the danger of comparison. As you perform, they will be thinking about the last person that presented the same material. How did they do it? How does your interpretation differ? Which one is better? You don't want them thinking about anything other than you. To hedge your bet, you should select monologues that are new and fresh to their ear. Show them something new that is a perfect fit for just you. Something, that they can only imagine you performing. It should show what you can do emotionally, intellectually and physically and most importantly be brief and to the point. Brief and to the point means about one to two minutes. Remember, your performance is a sample of what you can do, not the whole performance. If they want a whole performance, they need to cast you or buy a ticket.

Shorter monologues are also great to use within an acting class. Like an audition, you want to bring into the class a short sample of your acting ability or to showcase a specific aspect of your talent. If your strong suit is emotional roles, prepare a short emotional monologue. If it's physicality, then prepare something that relies centrally upon your ability to move within the space. This is no secret. Acting teachers and students prefer shorter monologues for class presentations. Why? This allows both the teacher and the student the ability to focus on specific acting issues rather than restating them over and over again within a cumbersome presentation. Usually, your acting teacher (just like a casting director) pretty much knows what they need to work on with you after the first minute of your presentation. So, why not dazzle them with a presentation that's short and sweet. Give just enough to make them interested but leave them wanting for more. If you can do that, you are where you need to be.

This book contains seventy individual monologues that can be performed by male or female characters. There is an equal mix of comedy and drama and all are within the one to two minute time range. You might be thinking, which one is right for me? Find a piece that you can closely connect to either on an emotional or intellectual level. Put yourself in the space as the character and let the monologue do the rest of the work. Ultimately, the right monologue for you is one that they have never seen that showcases your unique talents. Think of an audition monologue as a means to end. As an audition piece, it's going to exhibit what you can do and where you would fit in to a particular company or agent roster. As a class exercise it's going to give your acting teacher a specific insight about who you are, your talents and what areas of acting you need to work on.

Lastly, monologues like everything else, are subject to our tastes and needs at any given moment. Don't be afraid to try many different monologues as your creative growth progresses or you feel you need to do something different. Make this book your source for the magic that you will do. Go back to it again and again whenever you feel there is a need for it.

WHAT IS A MONOLOGUE?

The American Heritage Dictionary defines a monologue as a long speech made by one person, often monopolizing a conversation. You may be thinking, I already know that, tell me something I don't know. Okay, a monologue when spoken can reveal a small part of a character's soul. Think of those thoughts in which you have spoken aloud to someone or yourself. The words you speak come from within you and have special meaning. Unless, you count as monologues leaving phone messages, placing your order at the automated machine at Jack in the Box or trying to talk on the phone to customer service at your bank. It is true that a monologue is a speech made by one person but really it is a lot more than just that. What the person says in his/her speech should be worthy of speech itself to be considered a monologue. What am I saying? It should be a speech connected in some core way to your character's intellectual, emotional, spiritual and physical state. If it is not that, then it is not a monologue. It is whatever it is: leaving a phone message, ordering a cheeseburger or trying to find out why your check has bounced.

Within the framework of a performing arts presentation, a monologue is one person speaking for an extended period alone or with other characters upon the stage or within a camera shot. The speech can be the character's thoughts spoken aloud to himself or herself, to another character, to the audience or an object or entity. How a monologue is presented has a lot to do with the reality of the universe the character lives in and to a greater extent the point of view or creative framework of the presentation. I am defining point of view as **how** a creative work is presented to its audience. Several years ago, I attended a production of

William Shakespeare's Hamlet at small theatre in Los Angeles. I sat in the first row about three feet from the actor who played Hamlet as he uttered those famous lines **"To be or not to be..."** I had experienced this soliloquy dozens of times before within a representational framework where the Hamlet character reveals his inner thoughts by speaking to himself out loud. In this particular production, the actor who played Hamlet turned toward me and asked the famous question, **"To be or not to be?"** At first I wanted to blurt out like Robert Di Niro in **Taxi Driver, "Are you talking to me?"** But, somehow thought it might not be appropriate. So I said nothing. But, I did give him a look of acknowledgment. As if to say **"I heard that… and that is definitely a question to consider."** For the rest of the show, the audience kept looking at me as if they wanted me to do or say something. I never did. I am not saying that it was wrong to present the Hamlet soliloquy in this manner. The creative framework of that particular production of Hamlet was centered on the characters (including Hamlet) acknowledging the presence of the audience. At that particular performance, I unwittingly assumed that role. I could have chosen to respond verbally to Hamlet, but I chose just to acknowledge his look. However, we can say that Hamlet acknowledging the audience in the middle of his soliloquy was done on purpose and was part of the creative framework of the presentation. The creative framework, which defines a presentation of a play or film to an audience, usually falls within the point of view of the Director.

The Director sets the framework and tone of how the material will be presented. When you choose to perform a particular monologue, just like a director, you must choose **how** you will convey the reality of your character and situation to an audience. You must ask yourself, what do I want to achieve within my creative framework and what is the desired outcome? I am not suggesting that you perform your audition monologue directly to an auditioner. I think it is best to create a framework that keeps them separate from the reality of your character. This allows them the freedom to make notes on your performance, sit back and see what you can do. You don't want them; feeling forced to react to your gaze or directed line toward them. It will make them uncomfortable and lessen your chance to showcase what you can do. Your creative framework in presenting your monologue should be focused on how to best present the reality of the character you have created and to connect that character to your individual talents. The purpose of an audition monologue is not to solely entertain, it is to show how you create a character, interpret lines and present them to an audience.

Now that we have discussed what a monologue is and how it should be presented, let's get back to our original question. Why do we have to do monologues anyway?

WHY DO I HAVE TO DO A MONOLOGUE?

Most casting directors, when reading actors for a particular project, like to have the work performed from a specific script either as a cold reading or a memorized screen test. So having one or more monologues prepared is not going to land you a specific role in a film or television program. In order to do that, you are going to have to do a **cold reading** of the material from the project. If you cannot use a monologue for a film or television audition, why bother working on one?

The answer to the question of why we do monologues is to be able to show a casting person, agent or performing arts school representative our ability to perform prepared (rather than cold) material and offer such monologues within a clear-cut presentational format. In this book, I have developed primarily shorter pieces to be used for auditions and acting classes. In a classroom / studio setting, an actor can work on specific challenges of character creation, line memorization, nervousness and physicality. As an audition piece, the performer wants to present a monologue that is a concise sample of his/her work which highlights their ability to memorize dialogue, create the intellectual, emotional, physical and spiritual state of a character. It should also exhibit the actor's creative ability to present prepared material from a specific point of view. The **"how" and "why"** we do monologues then is clear. This is a sample of how you can interpret material when you have had a time to prepare it and present it within a specific creative framework. However, just because it is prepared, you are not expected to create a whole play. What is expected is for you to provide a short sample (one to two minutes) of your creativity and talent to a specific audience. Who is this audience? It can be an agent, producer, and an artistic director of a theatre ensemble, an admissions committee at an acting school/college or a director. However, the **who** is not as important as the **how** you create it. The first step in this process is the selection of the right material.

HOW DO I SELECT A MONOLOGUE THAT IS RIGHT FOR ME?

By Casting Type

No matter how versatile you think you may be as a performer, a casting director or agent will only see you playing roles that they feel fall within your appropriate casting type. Casting type is a combination of factors which can include your: age, physical stature, hair color, ethnicity, speech patterns or accent and generally the way you appear to most people most of the time. You want to select a monologue that is **type appropriate** for you. That is, if you are female age twenties, you should not select a character that is an older woman. Pick a character that is generally your own age. Agents and casting directors will look to identify you in one type category or another.

By talent and skills

If you are preparing a monologue for an audition for entrance into a school or theatre ensemble, you want to select material that will highlight what you do the best. If you have difficulty in showing intense emotion, then stay away from those types of monologues until you can perfect the skill to perform them. Select monologues that will highlight what you do best. Note that some schools require selection of monologues from existing plays either from a specific list or within a date range. For example, they may request preparation of two monologues: one classical such as Shakespeare, Moliere, or Sophocles and one contemporary within the last fifty years. If you are doing a short monologue for a commercial agent, select something contemporary no longer than two minutes. If you feel your strongest talent is comedy, then lead with that. If you feel your strongest talent is drama, then lead with that. Often, when you are requested to do two, they will have you perform the first one and then tell you the second monologue is not necessary. This does not mean that you have done a poor job. It just means that they have seen what they need to see.

Compatibility with career or artistic goals

Select monologues that are compatible with the goals you are attempting to achieve. If you are auditioning for a commercial agent, a crisp, short, high-energy (but not too happy) monologue would probably be best. A longer dramatic narrative or verse monologue would not be the best choice for a commercial agent, but may work in perfectly for an audition for a theatrical agent (film and television), theater company or college performing arts program.

Purpose or Skill Goal

An acting teacher may ask you to select a monologue, so that you can work on a specific acting goal such as anger, physicality or listening. For example, if you are asked to work on a specific emotion, select a monologue that will stretch your abilities in that area.

DON'T JUST RATTLE THROUGH A SPEECH - TREAT YOUR MONOLOGUE AS IF IT WERE A SCENE

Many actors hate performing monologues because they feel it is just a speech and not a true representation of their acting ability. They believe that performing a monologue does not provide the opportunity to show a casting director or agent the actor's ability to react to another character. We have stated earlier that a monologue is a longer speech where a character can speak to himself or herself, another character or object or the audience. When you create your monologue know **who** you are talking to and don't forget to create their presence for the audience. Your monologue dialogue should not be just a wall-to-wall recitation of lines but instead a well thought out pattern of dialogue, which takes into consideration the intellectual, emotional, physical and spiritual universe of the character.

Let's stop here a moment and define these four character attributes.

Intellectual:

This is what your character intellectually believes within his/her universe. It goes to the core of the things they do. It could be as simple as Democrat or Republican but it can go deeper about their understanding of the world they live in. Characters are often thrust into situations that force them to make decisions based upon logic rather than emotion.

This is often the case in business decisions where statistics or numbers are involved. However, an intellectual choice can also be based upon a belief system within the character. Some factor causes them to calculate and then act upon a decision that is centered around facts and data rather than feelings.

Emotional:

This is what your character feels about themselves and the other character they relate to in their universe. What emotion dominates their existence and how does it effect what they do and what happens to them. Certain situations demand an emotional response. What you feel becomes more important than what your character thinks or intellectually rationalizes in a given situation. In 1916, there was a shark attack on a little boy in an inland Florida lagoon. It was unbelievable to think that a shark would swim that far inland from the ocean. But it happened. As the shark attacked the seven year old, an adult man jumped into the water and attempted to pull him to safety. The shark killed them both, but there is more to it than that. The underlying motivation for the rescuer was to save the boy despite the danger of being torn apart himself. Perhaps it was fear itself that drew the man into the water. In either case, it was a totally emotional response.

Physical:

How does your character physically interact with the universe they live in? How do they move? How do they interact physically with other characters? Much of our physical response to the world is filtered through our culture and the times we live in. You could be on a subway car in New York City just inches away from another individual. Actually so close to them that you could smell what they ate for breakfast and not think anything of it because the physicality of that space and situation makes it so. You could take the same physical situation and place it on a line at the supermarket in Los Angeles and you would perceive anyone that close to you as invading your space. A character's physical interaction with the universe that surrounds them can also be influenced by culture or time period. What is acceptable in one culture or time period may not be acceptable in another.

Spiritual:

This goes beyond religious conviction to the core of your character's belief system. Your character's moral core and how they perceive what is right and wrong within their universe. Certain characters find themselves on a journey of discovery and their motivation is centered on that journey. Certainly, Don Quixote's quest in Man of La Mancha would be an example. But, your character doesn't have to be on a life long quest to find the meaning of life to have a spiritual motivation. The spirituality can simply be an exploration of aspect of your character's inner being.

Certainly, try to allow whom ever your character is speaking to react to what is being conveyed just as you would in a two-person scene. Your character speaks the lines in the monologue and then allows the other character or the audience to respond. Even if they are not making a sound, you need to give them time to react. If you do this, your presentation will be more than a mere recitation of the words of the script in which you race through the lines before you forget them. Allow whomever you are speaking absorb what you are saying and doing. In addition, don't forget to create them in the space. Look at them, react to them and allow them to react to what your character is doing within the piece.

WHAT'S THE BEST WAY TO MEMORIZE MY LINES AND CREATE A PHYSICAL LIFE FOR MY CHARACTER?

I have heard many actors complain: ***"I knew the lines outside but now, on the stage, I just can't remember anything."*** When I hear this type of statement, I know what they have forgotten to do is create a physical life for their character. They fall into the trap of thinking about a monologue as just a speech rather than a slice of a character's life. This means that the moment that we experience your character speaking, it is part of a much larger mosaic. When preparing to perform a monologue don't forget to create the physical life of the character. What I mean is the physical connection to where your character is and what they are doing as they speak. Creating a physical life will go a long way in helping you to memorize the lines. Your ability to memorize what your character is saying will be connected to a specific physical reality and idea. Your brain will connect what is being said to a specific movement and place. However, you cannot move without purpose. What kind of universe does your character live in and how do they move within it? A character's universe has everything to do with the actual space from which they speak, the time period they live in and the **who** they are speaking with. If your monologue is a soliloquy, which takes place in a graveyard, and your character is speaking aloud to themselves, this is different from a speech talking to your best friend over a cup of coffee.

PERFORMING A MONOLOGUE FOR AN AUDITION - HOW TO CREATE AN IMPLEMENTATION STRATEGY.

Think of an implementation strategy as a plan to create a frame or foundation to build your monologue. The implementation strategy becomes the concept for presentation. Whatever the purpose of your monologue your preparation for presentation should include an implementation strategy. You may think it is the director's job to create the framework of the character's physicality and emotion and that you should not have to concern yourself with the details of how it will be presented. The truth is that the **who and the how** are indelibly connected. It is like the chef who labors over the preparation and ingredients making up a particular dish, forgetting presentation and just throwing his creation onto a paper plate. In that very act, the chef negates the creative process that taken place before. An actor is no different; consideration of presentation is just as important as character preparation. While an actor cannot control all aspects of presentation, the development of an implementation strategy will create a foundation for the actor to rely upon.

CREATING A PERFORMANCE DYNAMIC - HOW TO MAKE A CREATIVE BOX TO PLAY IN

The dynamic of any presentation takes into consideration all of the physical characteristics of the performance space, the performer's relationship to that space, the distance of the intended audience to the performer, the composition of the intended audience, the surrounding reality of the performance and ultimately the purpose of the performance itself. The dynamics of any given performance can change as the physical characteristics of the space change. While it is virtually impossible for any performer to know totally the dynamic of every audition performance in advance, it is possible to develop a strategy of presentation, based upon what elements are available.

For an audition, you can only assume the dynamics of the space and distance to the intended audience. You might be asked to present your monologue in an office setting, a conference room, or an empty stage. The best strategy is to develop a plan for all three and be prepared for any variation you might encounter. In an audition dynamic, the person you are auditioning for may be looking for a specific element and not your total performance. They also may be multi tasking (making notations, conferring with an associate or looking at your resume) while you are in the midst of your performance. Lastly, the reality you attempt to create might be interrupted by an outside source such as a telephone, people entering the space or the casting person themselves.

HOW TO PLAY EACH MOMENT AS IF IT WERE A PIECE OF A LARGER MOSAIC

The **Presentation Dynamic** is literally the creative box you get to play in. It is the creative framework, which is made up of your character's world, and the actual physical elements within your specific performance environment all rolled into one. It could be a stage, a camera angle, a casting office, or on set location that your character must evolve within. Once you have established this creative framework, there is a multitude of possibilities that are present within that dynamic at that particular moment in time.

USING "WHAT IF?"

You have made the choices detailing **who, what, where and when**. Now, let your character ask him/herself the question: "**What If**" one of these choices weren't so? Example: You are Romeo quietly watching Juliet standing on her balcony.

Who:	A Montague (who falls in and out love) and enemy of the Capulet's
What:	Spying upon Juliet as she speaks her private thoughts
Where:	The Capulet's orchard, Verona - a place he should not be.
When:	Nighttime after the Capulet feast.

Romeo sees the love of his life but cannot muster the will to speak. As she speaks each line, he falls deeper and deeper into silence. He succumbs to his fear and gets up to run away when at the last possible moment, despite his fear, he hears Juliet say:

Romeo, doff thy name,

And for that name which is no part of thee

Take all myself!

When Romeo hears this, his fear, vanishes in an instant, and he speaks! Why? He knows he can get it all.

I take thee at thy word:

Call me but love, and I'll be new baptized;

Henceforth I never will be Romeo

Using the "**What if**," you are choosing to play the moment as if this time it will be different. You are playing this scene and speech as if he were going to walk away and somehow this play, at this moment in time is different than any other that has happened before. The key to playing the "**what if**" is that your character must believe it and more importantly the audience must believe that the "**what if**" is going to change the outcome. Fight the logical inclination to say to yourself, **this is Shakespeare or this is the text, it cannot be changed**. I am not suggesting a change in text, only a change in intention. We often play the end of the scene because there is a preconceived notion by both performers and audiences as to how it all turns out. We need to recreate that notion in the form of "**what if.**"

Let the audience sit on the edge of their seats and wonder if that maybe just this time, at this moment, Romeo just might walk away. What would happen then? Using this approach makes your work unpredictable and interesting.

HOW TO CREATE THE "MOMENT BEFORE"

Where have you come from and what has just happened the moment before?

Within the reality of your character, what moment has the character just left before they entered the moment of your monologue? What was significant about that moment and how has the moment before influenced the intellectual, emotional, physical and spiritual state of your character during the monologue? Within this creative framework, the actor then can convey the thoughts of the character, as they would appear in the full presentation of the work. Playing the moment before the lights go up or the camera rolls then allows the audience to catch your character in the midst of their existence living their life in its entirety.

HOW TO CREATE "NOW" USING SPECIFIC OBJECTIVES AND BEATS

What is your character's main objective?

By speaking the words of the monologue and living the moment, what does your character desire to have happen when they finish speaking? Ask yourself, **why** is my character saying and doing this? What is your character's desired outcome?

What are your character's sub objectives? Mark them as individual beats.

Are there smaller objectives or beats your character must overcome in order to achieve their main objective? A beat could be a small section of the dialogue or movement within the monologue. Create a series of beats within your monologue to identify your sub objectives. For example, what would Romeo's sub objectives be?

Beat #1	Romeo sees the love of his life but cannot muster the will to speak.
Beat #2	As she speaks, he succumbs to his fear and gets up to run away.
Beat #3	At the last possible moment, despite his fear, he hears Juliet say:

> **Romeo, doff thy name,**
>
> **And for that name which is no part of thee**
>
> **Take all myself!**

Beat #5	He stops. When Romeo hears this, his fear, vanishes in an instant.
Beat #6	He speaks.

> **I take thee at thy word:**
>
> **Call me but love, and I'll be new baptized;**
>
> **Henceforth I never will be Romeo**

What are the obstacles in the way of achieving your objectives?

In the course of events leading up to, during and after the completion of the monologue, can you identify any obstacles, which are preventing your character from achieving his/her desired goals? Are these obstacles generated externally (literally physical elements) or internal (obstacles created from within your character) which prevent them from their objective? Identify these obstacles and create ways to acknowledge and overcome them.

What is going on at this moment?

At the very moment the monologue begins, what is actually happening? If you took a snapshot of this moment, what would be its title? If you enter the your home holding a bouquet of flowers, kiss your wife and hand them to her, and then after giving them to her, you tell her that you have lost your job, what is the title you would place under this moment? It can be called many things, perhaps "**losing my job**" or "**loss**" but it would not be called "**Handing her the bouquet**" because that action is not what is really going on. It is just an action, which is part of the overall moment. So ask yourself, what is really going on in your character's universe at the moment your monologue begins.

When is this moment in time?

Once you have established what the true moment is, then address the question is "**when**" is it? Using the example described above, the moment can be described as morning, day or night but more helpful would be the moment after I lost my job or late at night after I have been walking for hours, because I didn't know how I would tell you. It is literally a definition of "**now**." Once you understand this, you will know what to play. But also understand that "**now**" is constantly changing as the moment evolves.

Where are you? What is the space for your character?

Even though you may perform your monologue in any number of nondescript spaces, make a decision for your character about specifically where this moment is taking place. Is it at home, on the bus, in an elevator, on a podium in front of a thousand spectators? What is the space? Is it small and confined, larger than life or somewhere in between? Do not confuse this with the Dynamic of Performance (that is more concerned with the physical properties of the performance space) the "**where are you**" question addresses solely the reality of the character's universe rather than the performance space. Make specific decisions about the space your character occupies when they begin to move and speak.

HOW TO CREATE THE "MOMENT AFTER"

Where are you going?

If your character is in a particular space in a particular moment, where will they go next? Is it somewhere specific? Create a concept of motion. Let your words in the monologue and the physical life you have in the moments you create propel you to the next.

Everybody likes to know where they have been and where they are going

I am not asking you to predict the future. However, your character and the audience, in a larger sense, should have some idea about where your character is going intellectually, emotionally physically and spiritually as a result of the monologue being spoken. Everybody loves to peer into the future and know, if even briefly, what the next moment will bring. Even if you don't really have a clear-cut idea of all of it, give your character and your audience a taste of what may come next. An audience, will say, **"Okay, I have watched and listened to you, now what's going to happen?"** Answer the question: **"Now that I have spoken these words, this is what's going to happen next."** You have to show them how it's going to be and take them along with you on your journey.

"What has happened during this journey?" After all that has been said, has your character changed? If your character has spoken aloud to himself or herself another character or the audience, has this auditory expression of their inner thoughts changed them in anyway? It may be a minute change, but it is a change nonetheless. What happens next? You as the performer and your character have to answer the question: How has the universe changed and because of that change what will happen next? You do not have to write new lines to your monologue but there has to be a sense that something will follow.

How do you play this?

We have come full circle. Your character must have some resolve intellectually, emotionally, physically and spiritually that connects to what is going on within their universe.

How do you show this?

The way your character contemplates on what they have just spoken in the monologue, or how they react emotionally, or how they physically accommodate the change. Your monologue does not end when the character utters the last line. It ends when the audience experiences the character's reaction to the last line. The audience wants a sense of the significance of what has transpired and glimpse of what will be. That is what keeps them invested in your character, they want to know and be part of what is going to happen next.

When Macbeth speaks the last few lines of his soliloquy, the audience has had a glimpse of his tormented soul and has seen the shadow of the murder that is to come.

Macbeth

I have no spur to prick the sides of my intent,

but only vaulting ambition,

which o'erleaps itself and falls on the other

When Macbeth utters the last line **"And falls on the other,"** the very moment after, we see the murder that is to take place within his eyes. He exits with a resolve that is clear to us all when he walks off the stage. The audience knows, he has changed and because of this resolution, something significant is going to happen. He is going to kill the king and we have witnessed the creation of this decision.

HOW TO BEGIN A MONOLOGUE AT AN AUDITION

You have done your preparation, what about the audition itself? When you enter the audition space, get a sense of the room. What is the energy level of the people inside? Where are they sitting? In front of you, on the side or both? How large is the space? What is the distance between where you will perform and the people watching you? What is the acoustic quality of the space? Where is the light and are there any seats or other set materials in the space? Adjust to any deficiencies on the fly. If it is a stage and there is an object in your way from a previous audition, it is okay to use it or move it out of the way. Try to make the space as accommodating for your performance as you can. Make the space your own as you create the universe of your character.

If you are required to speak before, you perform your monologue or do a verbal set up which might include the monologue title and a little bit of background about the source material and setting, try to be as concise as possible. Try not to use words like **"um" or "like."** Instead, be very specific and state the name of the source material and a short summary of the portion of the source material that you are performing and what (if anything) is unique about it. You can prepare this in advance and memorize as part of the overall presentation. If the situation calls for you to go right into your monologue take your time to create the universe that your character lives in. Once it is time to start the actual performance portion of your audition, make sure you allow some time to separate the reality of the **"audition"** and the reality of the **"universe of the character"** you are to perform. Don't be a **good soldier** and go directly from an interview into a character. You will not totally achieve the transition and your performance will seem uneven and full of distractions. Before you speak, take a moment to let your character's universe surround you. Don't do warm ups, stretch out or lower your head toward the floor as you **get into character** then suddenly face forward as the character in a totally different physicality. This caveat may seem elementary but I have seen actors do it all the time.

Remember that your monologue does not begin with your first line. It begins with the moment before the first line, which causes your character to say those words. A monologue can even begin with a physical action or creation of an emotional or physical state by the character. If you are playing Hamlet, ask yourself what causes this character to speak the line **"To be or not to be..."** He just doesn't speak those words because Shakespeare wrote them. There is an underlying moment that occurs before the lines are spoken that drives the character to speak those words. When your character speaks those first words of your monologue, let them be a reaction to a previous intellectual, emotional or physical moment. This can be a previous moment in the play, film, or something the audience has not even seen. How you play this reaction to a previous moment has all to do with your character's intellectual, emotional, physical and spiritual connection. Ask yourself the question, what does my character ***"think"*** about this situation, how does my character ***"feel"*** right now and how does my character respond ***"physically"*** to this place and situation at hand. And what are your character's beliefs about the nature of their universe and what is right and what is wrong? Once you have answers to these questions, you will have something to play.

WHO SHOULD I LOOK AT WHEN I PERFORM AN AUDITION MONOLOGUE?

Your character can speak to themselves aloud, to another character or to the audience. However, most individuals involved within the casting selection process do not like to be included in the reality of the presentation. They want to be free to make notes and just experience what you are doing. Some acting teachers direct their students to speak **over the heads** of their audience. I don't like this practice because it is distracting to watch and does not allow the auditioner to connect to your character. Better, if you are directing your monologue as a soliloquy, direct your comments and actions to yourself. If you are speaking to another character, create a space for that character that the auditioner can easily see. This can be an empty space on the stage or a chair or set piece. If you are addressing the audience, create a similar empty space or spaces within the audience area. In this way, the auditioner can choose to participate when they want to but also be free to look down and make notes about you or your performance. Ultimately, I am not one for rules, if you perform your monologue directly to the auditioner, you will not fall through a hole in the floor. You can do anything you want to do to create the best reality for your specific monologue.

HOW DO I END MY AUDITION MONOLOGUE?

In a typical production setting, when your monologue is completed the lights might fade or another character might speak. In a film, another character can speak; they could cut to the next scene or fade to black. In an audition setting, you will not have any control over the space in which you will perform. There may be harsh lighting; exterior noise or it may not be a performance space at all. I have seen several methods of ending a monologue that I suggest that **you not do.** The first, at the end of the monologue, the actor just bows their head toward the floor as if to say, **"its over – you can applaud now."** As you can imagine this unnatural ending is abrupt and solicits an artificial applause and response from your auditioner. Applause belongs in a theatre performance, not an audition. The second method, at the end of the monologue the actor says the word **"scene."** This is a verbal cue spoken to the auditioner indicating that the monologue is over. This method is unnatural and creates an abrupt almost jarring quality. In addition, actors who use this method of ending have a tendency to physically comment upon their work when they say **"scene."** They complete their monologue and then in a very different physicality shrug their shoulders upward in apology and say **"scene."** This is not a monologue ending; it is an apology. It is as if the actor says to the auditioner, **"I'm so sorry for making you sit through this awful monologue."** All of these artificial methods don't allow the monologue to end naturally. What then, should you do?

If we operate on the assumption that you are not directly addressing your auditioner during your monologue, then ending your monologue is very simple. You complete the last line or action of the monologue and then allow a moment after to occur. This allows both the audience and whomever your character is speaking to react to that last moment. You take this short beat, then change your physicality from your character's **back** to your own or neutral position and look directly at and acknowledge the auditioner. This will tell them that the reality created for the character has now ended and that you are back at the audition. You don't ask for applause or any reaction for that matter.

All you are communicating to the auditioner is that the monologue is now over. The auditioner normally will say **"thank you"** and that is it. They may comment on your performance, give specific notes or ask you additional questions. Remember, it is not a good idea to comment on your own performance because it is a losing proposition either way. If you say, **"Wow, that was terrible. I can't believe how bad that was."** They may not have felt that way. Alternatively, if you say, **"Wow, was that hot or what? I can't believe how well I just nailed it today."** In this case, they may also not agree. Best bet is to not comment at all and let them do the talking. If you are asked to perform portions again and are given notes, listen to them carefully and try to incorporate them into your second performance. Many times an auditioner will give notes just to see how you take direction and incorporate their comments into your performance.

HOW TO HAVE FUN AT AN AUDITION

This last note will sound a bit cliché' but if you are having a good time your auditioner will be more likely to become engaged in the intellectual, emotional, physical and spiritual life of your character. In addition, if you feel good about what you are doing, you will do it better. Can you visualize that first moment you had the thought that you wanted to be an actor? Maybe you were watching television, a movie or a play. You sat in your seat and you thought to yourself.

"I can do that! I want to be up there on the screen or on the stage. I want to do it because it's something I enjoy. No it's something that I love. I love to act because it's inside of me and part of who I am. I can't think of doing anything else!"

Okay, so that seems a bit over the top. But didn't you ever feel this way at least a little bit. Well, I want you to go back to that personal moment for you. Go back to it and remember that you wanted to act because you love it and it makes you happy when you do it. Keep that always in your heart and find joy in what you do. Even if you don't get the part or you get it wrong, it doesn't matter because there will always be another day, another audition and another part to play. When you audition or perform in class, have a great time. Be thankful that you have the opportunity to perform and share your talent with someone. This is not really advice, its common sense. But it goes to the core of why we act. We act because we love to act and that passion should be part of everything that we do.

THE MONOLOGUES

#1 CONFESSIONS OF A SERVER

I can't believe it.

The couple sitting at table seven is losing it big time. She just threw a glass of Cabernet in his face and his shirt now looks like a Rorschach test. At the rate they're going, they won't make dessert. I got the whole story when I brought their third round of drinks. She looked up at me and snapped, **"He told me he would divorce his wife – what a crock! That was five years ago!"** I didn't know what to say. Then, she grabbed my arm. **"Do I look like an idiot to you? Well Do I?"** I said, of course not, would you like to hear about our specials tonight?" She just continued. **"Well, he thinks I'm an idiot!"** Then she let him have it. The whole glass of seventeen dollar a glass Cab. For a second, I thought he was going to toss his glass back at her. What can you say when something outrageous like that happens? I smiled politely and said, **"Let me check on your appetizers... I'll be right back."**

(Beat)

Shit.... This job is getting dangerous.

#2 LAUNDRY

Let's face it... it's my own fault. When they called me and said they wanted me to work on campus today, I was so excited that I forgot to ask how much they were paying. I figured it was eighteen an hour and that's not bad when you figure all you have to do is sit here behind this table and smile at every guy/babe that passes by. I mean I'm an actor right? I should be able to do that. It's pure and simple... just selling. But what am I selling? Nothing very sexy. My job is to get (mostly guys) to sign up for a laundry service. You know, the service they provide is to pick up your dirty clothes and bring them back to you all clean in a bundle. That's it! Not very challenging for an aspiring actor like myself... but it's a clean job (no pun intended) and I can make my own hours so I have time to audition... so that's good right. But the real rip is they're only paying me ten bucks an hour! I wonder if they're going to take tax out of that?

#3   RESCUE

Let me tell you something about myself... I rescue animals. Any kind of animal a mouse, a snake, a bird... if they're in trouble, I rescue them. Well, the truth is I have never rescued anything but cats and dogs. If I see one walking down the street all by itself. I pick it up, take it home, give a bath, feed it and find it a home. That's what I do... there's a need for it. There was this white cat sitting in the middle of the road the other day that almost got run over by a truck. I picked it up and held it in my arms just in a nick of time. I was taking it back to my car, when outta nowhere, this old lady took a swing at me with her cane. She called out to me **"Son of a bitch! You're kidnapping my little Snowball!"** I put little Snowball back on the ground and he took off. How the hell was I supposed to know? Just as she pinned me to the wall with the sharp part of her cane, a cop car pulled up. That old lady would have stabbed me with that thing if those cops didn't come to my rescue.

#4   HOLD DOWN THE SEATS

When we go to the movies and sit down, why is it that I'm always the one that has to get up again, go to the concession counter and buy you a drink and popcorn? I know you would go... but you can't... because YOU have to hold down the seats.

Hold down the seats... what does that actually mean? You're holding down the seats from whom? You make it sound like we are at war and you have to hold down the seats so these velvet-coated masterpieces don't fall into enemy hands. While I, the brave soldier, venture across enemy lines to get supplies. Just once, I'd like you to get the Diet coke and popcorn. I'll even pay for it, if that's what you're worried about.

Just once, I would like to HOLD DOWN THE SEATS.

#5   SITTING SOMEWHERE OUTSIDE

What a beautiful night sky. I just love to look at the stars and wonder about the universe... my life.... and... us. When I say us... I mean you and me... together. It's just a beautiful picture isn't it? However, one thing could make it better.... The night air is a little chilly and I was wondering if I could borrow your sweater? I know what you're thinking... Why didn't I dress in layers so I would have my own sweater to wrap around my shoulders? But the truth is... I just didn't have anything to go with this outfit... and now I'm chilly. No, I'm cold! So fashion just went out the window in favor of just keeping warm. You can understand that can't you? But you still haven't offered it to me. Maybe you're thinking, this is the only way I'm going to learn to be more responsible? I'll freeze this time but will know better next time. Something like that.

(Beat)

You don't look like you want to give that sweater up do you? So I'll tell you what, we can take your sweater and wrap it around both of us. Wouldn't that be nice?

(Beat)

Wouldn't it? **Well wouldn't it?**

(Beat)

No? No, no, no... I'll be just fine. Just fine...

(Folds her arms tightly and looks up at the night sky.)

#6   THE CLEANSE

I was listening to the radio yesterday and there was this commercial which went on endlessly about cleansing your body by drinking raw veggie juice... which they were more than happy to sell you... and the claim... if you drank it four times a day and didn't eat anything else for a whole week... that you would lose weight (maybe 20 pounds) and be healthier.

(Beat)

I mean really, if you don't eat anything for a week of course you're going to get skinny. But then what? You lose a whole bunch of weight, probably are miserable and more importantly you're hungry! Not to mention, you have to buy all new clothes... what good is all that?

#7   SPIRIT

    Sometimes and only sometimes… at night when it's quiet, I can sense your presence. It's not like a scary thing. It's just that one part of me feels warmer than the rest of my body and I imagine that it's you… trying to touch me. When that happens, I can smell your hair… just the way it used to smell just after you washed it when it was still wet and you were right next to me. You are there again… just for an instant. Then, you're gone. I know it's you doing this… you hide my keys in the kitchen drawer… I don't get mad because I know you're just playing a joke on me… and sometimes… I hear your voice softly whisper my name in the dark.

    (Beat)

    …and just sometimes and only sometimes… in the shadows… from the corner of my eye… I can see your spirit… for a brief moment…

You are just the way you were

(Beat)

and you are with me again.

#8   CONFESSIONS OF A SERVER - *NEVER ORDER FISH ON A SUNDAY*

There's this couple back there on table four and I can just tell that it's a first date. You know, the way they're smiling at each other and nodding affirmatively at almost everything. How cute! You can just tell that they're both hitting it off and it's going perfectly. And I'm going to try to make a special night for them. I definitely will steer them away from the **Chef's Special.** A **Chef's Special** is a restaurant's creative way of selling you the food that's left over from the day before. In our case… it's meat loaf… and let me tell you… you don't want to know what's in it. And speaking of the day before or even longer… I'll keep these two lovebirds away from the supposed *"fresh"* fish. It's Sunday and we haven't had a fish delivery since Friday… so the fish is what can I say? Fishy? Hey, that's almost funny… there's something *"fishy"* about the fish!

(Beat)

But seriously, never order a Chef's Special or fish on Sunday… if you don't want to be sick or with explosive diarrhea on Monday. It's a known fact in the restaurant world.

(Beat)

Well gotta go! The little lovebirds are calling me over… I just know these two are gonna make a great couple!

#9　CONFESSIONS OF A SERVER – THE BAD TIPPER

Well… well… well… look who just walked in… "Mr. asshole!" The hostess is putting him right where I want him… in the back next to the men's room. The last time he was here he left me two bucks on an eighty-dollar check! And now he's back… and it's payback time.

You know servers are like elephants… we never forget. You can screw us once… but you won't get away with it a second time. There he is now… reading the menu. I'm gonna get him real good this time. First, I'll make his tongue hang out before I bring him a glass of water… and the water is coming from the men's toilet. He'll ask me for bread… and he'll get it… after I pat my armpits with each piece. I won't even mention what I'm gonna do to the bread sticks. For the main course, I'm gonna have a homeless guy who sleeps in the alley sneeze on it before I bring it to him.

I will burn that mother f….

(Beat)

Please don't think ill of me. I was only kidding.

(Smile)

I was just thinking… what I might do if he orders the cream pie…

#10 THANK YOU

Well... thank you for a great evening. I think it's important for people to say **"thank you"** to one another. There is so little civility left in this world.

I'm so sorry that I didn't wear a costume. When you said, **"dress up,"** I thought you meant... **dress "up!"** Well, that's why I'm wearing this (F) dress / (M) suit instead of jeans. I mean, I didn't want you to think I wasn't listening to you. I had no idea you wanted me to wear a costume. Actually, I have no idea of what I would have worn? I am so so sorry about that misunderstanding on my part.

I can't tell you how impressed I am with your (M) GREEN HORNET... (F) WONDER WOMAN What? Sorry (M) BATMAN / (F) TOMB RAIDER outfit... I mean costume. I especially love the blinking lights around each of your breasts. Reminds me of Christmas. Oh? That's chest armor?

There I go again... I just can't get anything right tonight. And while I'm apologizing, I wanted to tell you how truly sorry I am for spilling that strawberry margarita on your cape. It was an accident. If the picture your friends took of you is posted on Facebook, I'm sorry for that as well.

(Beat)

Well... thank you again... no need to walk me to the door. I'm good.

Really. Just, thank you.

#11 WOMAN'S WORK – CLEANING (MALE)

As a general rule I don't clean. I mean I take a shower every morning – well, most mornings. When I have time… and **if** it's not too cold outside… or if I don't get up too late.

If it's one of those **non-shower** days, I just do the under the arm thing and I'm out the door. But, I digress.

I don't clean the place I live in. Never have. I use what I call the ebb and flow technique. I move stuff from one place to another to give it a different look. But cleaning… guys do not clean.

(Proud stance)

We're men.

We hunt.

We gather.

We ebb we flow

Women clean.

(Beat… sniffs his shirt)

Pretty nasty...

Well, I guess today is one of those... **non-shower days**

Bet I can still get one more wearing out of this baby

Then I'll throw it out... go to the mall

and hunt me up another.

#12 WOMAN'S WORK – CLEANING – (FEMALE)

What is it with my boss? I can always tell when he doesn't shower. You can smell it as soon as you walk in the office. The sweet smell of manly fragrance… **ode de toilet** hits you like a ton of bricks falling out of a ten-story window. You say to yourself **he probably got up late… and did the under the arms thing**. But you know the real truth is that he is just a lazy loser who didn't bother to take a shower. So you pretend not to notice and get through the day.

(Beat)

I can say this now. Women are cleaner than men… I know men have that whole **hunter gatherer** excuse… but let's face it, when was the last time one of you guys ever had to hunt and gather anything? You just leave it all to us. We have to clean the house, clean the office and go to the store and we do the hunting and gathering to bring home food to cook for you. But no, that will never be… because you think to do any of that is just… **woman's work.** And that's the way it is and that's the way it will always be. But can you do me a favor?

Can you try taking a shower once in a while?

#13 DILLY DALLY

I'm one of those people that likes to get things done. Everyday, I make myself a list... and one by one, my favorite thing to do is to check things off of it. Did this. Check. Did that. Check! I love to say, **"check!"** The list gets shorter and I have a sense of accomplishment and mobility. I feel like I'm going from one point to another. **"Progressing."**

So the one thing that makes me crazy are people who waste time. You know who you are. You love to **"dilly dally"** your day away wandering from one point to another like the silver ball in a pinball machine. You start lots of things but never finish one of them. Why? I don't know? All I can say from observing is that you start something, and then get distracted by something else. So you drop one thing before it's completed and go onto the next. You are a tangled ball of incompletion! All you do is dilly dally...

The result is nothing and I mean nothing gets done. I just had to get that off my chest. Okay?

(Beat)

Check!

There, I feel better already!

(Exits)

#14 STEPPING ON THE CRACKS

The other day, I was walking on the sidewalk just doing an errand. Nothing important. I think it was a trip to the grocery store. I was halfway there when out of nowhere my right foot got caught on one of those cracks in the sidewalk – where one part of the sidewalk pops up. My foot got caught on that and down I went onto by elbow. At first, I just thought it was a little slip, but then about an hour later I couldn't bend my arm. Well, you guess it, I broke my elbow and now, as you can see, I have to walk around with my arm sticking out like this. I don't want you to think I'm just trying to get sympathy or that I'm a complainer because I'm not. But now, I find it hard to do the most mundane tasks like get dressed, drive a car, and take a shower… I can't bend my arm. How am I supposed to do anything!

Okay, I'm complaining.

A step shorter or one step longer and I would have walked right over that crack… then I wouldn't be in this situation. I think there's a lesson here… watch where you're going and make sure you don't step on any of those cracks!

#15 EMPLOYEE AT WILL

Yesterday at around 4:30 in the afternoon, I got called into the Human Resources office at my job. I should have known something was up when they called me to make sure I was on my way there. I don't think I had ever been to the Human Resources office since I first got my job about ten years ago. Back then, it was a quick stop just to fill out forms and then I never went back there again. That is, until yesterday. I was shown in to a small office – It was just a desk and a chair no pictures on the walls… just an empty room. A young guy wearing a tie and a very wrinkled shirt came out and sat down. I had never seen him before. He opened up a thin file folder and told me coldly that **the company** decided to let me go. That was it. I'm telling you that I never saw it coming. When I asked why?

He told me simply that I was an **"employee at will."** That meant that it was their right to let me go and of course it was my right to quit anytime I wanted. He offered his hand out to wish me the best. I put out my hand to return the gesture, but I just couldn't do it. Instead, I grabbed him by his tie pulled him slowly down until his head hit the desk. I didn't say a word, just turned and left. He said I was an **"employee at will"** and that was my will at that moment.

#16 SANITY

It's finally quiet… I don't think I could have taken another second of all the noise… our constant bickering and the slamming of doors. I hate the sound of a door slamming. It's so final. So closed to any possibility. It locks the energy into the room and prevents air from coming in. Now, it's darker, the lights are lower and I can feel the air circulating around me. I can feel each breath enter my body circulate then go back out again.

The quiet envelops me. I can almost hear my heart beat. There it is. And the tension in my chest is going away. Now it's darker and the quiet slowly surrounds me with a stillness I've never felt before. Not a sound… then blackness.

I'm finally at peace.

#17 VIETNAM AND THE FORT HAMILTON LAMENT

Now first of all, when I was a young man back in those crazy sixties there was a war going on in Vietnam. Most Americans, including myself, didn't give a rat's ass about what was happening over there. We were more interested in having fun... well the government had different ideas about what we should be doing and set up the draft. So, if you weren't rich or disabled you were going to be drafted and get an all expense paid trip to Vietnam. I got my notice to report to Fort Hamilton in Brooklyn, New York. I remember showing up there and having to strip down to my underwear so they could check me out. It was a humiliating experience, and when it was all said and done I found myself, still in my underwear, waiting on a long line. When it finally got to be my turn, a straight-faced sergeant stamped my papers and said **"1Y Rejected."** I was a little put back... thought I was in pretty good physical condition... then couldn't help but ask why. I said **"Why?"** He looked at me like I had a disease or something and said **"Flat feet! We'll call you if they attack Jones Beach. Now get the hell outta here!"** They pushed me out the front door like I was a piece of unwanted trash. After it was all over, I sat on the curb in front of Fort Hamilton looking down at my feet and wondering what I would do next.

#18 PALACE HOTEL– NEW YORK CITY

Check out this view! I'm on the 40th floor of the Palace Hotel looking out at the New York City skyline and below me I can see the roof of the Saint Patrick's Cathedral. As I look at the cathedral from above I realize that it is shaped just like a Christian cross. I wonder if they did that on purpose? Then, I look at all those people below moving around down there in the street. They look just like ants walking on a donut.

(Beat)

Makes you realize just how small we actually are. I mean small in comparison to our achievements. All these tall buildings… and cathedrals shaped like crosses… built by all those little people small as ants. Makes you stop and wonder.

#19 I'M NOT HERE RIGHT NOW

I realize I'm sitting right in front of you sipping a Martini. Yes, I'm on this stool and we're sitting at this bar and the man at the piano is playing the Frank Sinatra song **"Summer Wind."** The neon lights actually make you look beautiful. Especially the red… I just pretended to laugh at something you just said. But the truth is… I'm not here right now. I'm somewhere else. You gently touched my hand and smiled. I smiled back but really, I don't mean it. I don't want to hurt you. It's not you it's me…

(Beat)

Okay, that's not true. It **is** you. I've grown tired of you. Frankly everything about you. The way you look at yourself in the bar mirror as you gesture.

The way your perfume smells… like lilac and ginger ale.

And the high-pitched sound of your voice.

I just smiled again at something you said but I'm not sure I was supposed to?

But you probably didn't notice it anyway… so wrapped up in your own little narcissistic fantasy that you wouldn't even hear me if I screamed out loud.

So, go on… talk as long as you like. But the truth is… I am not here right now.

#20 HOW DEEP TO DIG A HOLE

When I was a little kid, I had this weird thing I would do. I used to bury my toys… pretty much like a dog buries a bone. I'm sure there's some sort of physiological explanation for it, but I can't tell you what it is. I would bury my toys so I would always know where they were and that they were safe. I struggled with making the decision about how deep I would have to dig to insure that the toy I was burying would remain undisturbed and safe. I thought, the deeper the hole, the safer whatever I was putting in it would be. But then I didn't want to dig so deep that I wouldn't be able to find it again. What good would that be?

When I think about it now, I'm probably still digging holes… not real holes but the emotional kind. I don't have many friends but when I care about someone, I like to know where they are. I want to keep them close and safe and don't want to share them with anyone else.

(Beat)

I moved away from my childhood home when I was only ten leaving behind everything I had ever buried there. I often wonder if all the toys I buried in those holes I dug when I was a kid are still there? And if someone found them, would they wonder how they got there.

(Beat)

If I ever get back that way, I should go knock on the door and ask.

#21 LISTENING

Have you ever pretended that you're listening to someone speaking when you're not? They're talking, their lips are moving – you hear them and look back in earnest. Sometimes you even nod in agreement while they're rattling away - talking about something you don't care about. They might even be complaining about the fact that no one ever listens to one word they say.   While **you** in your mind are snowboarding down a snowy white slope in Tahoe or catching a wave on a surfboard Hawaii.

(Beat)

And when they tap you on the arm and say, **"Are you listening to me?"** You reply, **"Absolutely!"** They smile back at you and continue… **"Blah Blah Blah"** and you… earnestly nod in agreement… then catch another wave.

#22 ARCHIPELEGO

    I've always had a problem connecting things intellectually. I need to visualize it all in piece or I can't understand it. I just can't comprehend things in pieces. Then, I'm too busy trying to put the pieces together to see how they fit rather than understanding them individually. I guess I'm like that with people too. I look at people like pieces of a puzzle and put them into neat little groupings that don't always fit together. There are the work people, my friends, acquaintances, and family. And then there's a pretty large group of people I don't like. I put them all in one place together. Whenever, I meet someone new, I assign them to one of these larger groupings even though sometimes they don't always fit.

    One major rule I have is to never mix the people from one group with another. I mean you wouldn't want to mix "friends" with "family." Just think about how disastrous that would be? Everybody needs to stay within their own group. It's so much easier than having to deal with an individual.

    Kind of like an archipelago instead of the island.

#23 PENELOPE CRUISE

I was driving around in my car last night with my girlfriend Penelope. Nothing big… we were just cruising around in my dad's car. Like we do almost every night. And every once in a while, we stop… for a little this… and a little that… ya 'know what I mean. A little **"chinga chonga."** Hey, what the fo? You gotta do what you gotta do… am I right? Then when we get hungry, we stop at IN & OUT for a few burgers and a milkshake. Then I have to get her back home before midnight.

(Beat)

Like I said, everything was going great then BAM outta nowhere… Penelope screams at me… to pull over just as we're passing the mall parking lot. I slam on the brakes and she jumps out of the car and tells me we were breaking up. Why you ask? She's says she's tired of doing nothing. Ya'know just cruising around all the time. I thought that's what she wanted to do? I even had a vanilla instead of chocolate shake at IN & OUT cause I thought she liked it. I hate vanilla.

But that was it. She slammed the car door I watched her walk across the mall parking lot and disappear through the glass doors of the food court. Maybe she was still hungry?

(BEAT)

So now… here I am… no more cruising with Penelope… what the fo… I just wish I had all that money I spent on gas.

#24 SHE LOOKS GREAT IN THE DARK

She looks great in the dark. I mean really hot. Her blondish hair touching her shoulders has a purplish glow from the neon beer sign hanging in the back of the bar. Her black jacket blends effortlessly with the black lacquered barstool and her legs wrapped in fishnet are folded under the bar ledge so tight I can't see them. But what I can see looks very inviting.

All I really can see is her face, her blue eyes and mostly her mouth. I find myself looking at her mouth a lot, especially when she speaks because I can't hear her voice over the loud music. Her long nails dipped in glossy red enamel gently rub against the top of my hand and she sips her vodka soda with a splash of cran.

She smiles at me. And I think to myself, **"She likes me!"**

Then I think again… this can't be right. This is way too easy and she's way to hot for me. Something's gotta be wrong here. She smiles at me again and this time holds my hand really tight.

I only hope she looks this great when they turn on the lights.

#25 BAD HAIR DAY

I don't know about you but I don't wash my hair everyday. Do you? I'm not even sure I should be saying this to you. It's kind of personal. Well, do you? Wash your hair every day? Okay, I can appreciate your unwillingness to share. But looking at it… up close… your hair looks a little flat. It doesn't have that fluffy just washed look. I'm not sure if you really want it that way or not. Please don't take this as criticism.

(Beat)

So, did you? Did you wash your hair?

(Beat)

You did?

(Beat)

No, it looks fine. Not really flat at all. Now that I look at it, it's kind of fluffy in the back. Yeah right there where it's sticking up… right next to the bald spot.

(Beat)

Hey, no sweat… it's not really **that** bald. Maybe pushed over to the side… too much. You might just be having a bad hair day.

#26 CRAZY ASS BEE

    I was sitting at the pool in my backyard yesterday. Sitting all peaceful in a dappled sunlight under an umbrella. Sipping a Pina Colada and thinking to myself, **"shit… life ain't so bad. At least today as I lay here stretching my legs out and closing my eyes."** Pretty nice thought eh? Then, I had this weird sensation that there was something crawling on my head. I reached up to scratch only to find that it was a bee. I flicked him off me and he landed right in my Pina Colada and stayed there long enough to have a few sips before I picked him out with a straw. I could've put him on the floor and crushed him with a magazine. But I thought, let the little guy live. When I put him down on the ground he flicked the pineapple juice off his wings and flew up and landed on my head again! I flicked him off again and he came right back to that same spot on my head. This time, he stung me. I pulled him off me and ripped his stinger out of my head. He fell to the floor, and after a minute he was dead. My head hurt a little but I really felt bad that the little guy had died. His persistence eventually destroyed him. I thought to myself, **"*crazy ass bee…*"** Then, took a sip of my drink stretched my legs out and went back to sleep.

#27 DOG PEOPLE AND CAT PEOPLE

Okay, I'll admit it. I'm a dog person. It doesn't mean that I don't like cats. Cats are cool but I relate to dogs better. Dog people tend to hang out together. They support one another in their "**doggedness.**" They are more co-dependent. They go to coffee shops and shopping malls with their canine friends seeking to connect with other dog people. Why? Dog people have an insatiable desire to connect and be validated. They need to be told they are okay and that their world is a happy place. Now, cat people… they just don't care. They are mostly loners. Have no real friends and pretend to be popular when the truth is… nobody likes them. Dog people carry pictures of their dogs around with them in their smart phones and wallets. They talk to their dogs as if they were humans and pretend they can answer them. "**See Skippy wag his tail? That means he wants his cappuccino with no foam.**" Cat people rarely take their feline counterparts anywhere. That's because a cat really has very little use for a human contact. Cats use humans for a modicum of shelter and food. Other than that, a cat could care less. Dogs are **needy** companions who constantly require the verbal praise of their masters. Dog people say they go to dog parks to have their pets socialize with other dogs. The truth is, dog people us their pets as a social lubricant to meet other dog people. Cat people just open the door and let them out not knowing **when** or **if** they will ever return.

Like I said, I'm one of those dog people constantly reaching out… and hoping… to connect… to someone… anyone… who is just like me.

#28 LIVING INSIDE A HEFTY BAG

Ever have somebody sit near you and the next thing you know they're coughing up something... awful, then sniveling all over you?

Like this...

(Cough up something)

And snivel

(Snivel)

When they do it, they sort of reach over toward you and then let it go. Why don't these people stay home if they're sick? Am I right? Nooooo! They have to be right next to you! Then, there's another cough and then a snivel and let's not forget the wipe. They wipe their nose with their bare hand and then dry it off by rubbing it on themselves or even worse a door handle or the arm of a chair. I'm telling you it's dangerous out there.

(Beat)

Next time I leave the house, I'm going to wrap myself in a Hefty bag.... And maybe then I'll stand a fighting chance.

#29 VISUAL AUDITORY

A true **realist** experiences the world objectively using their five senses. You know sight, touch, taste, smell and hearing. But, the truth is our senses are not all equal. Some of us are **visual** and connect to everything they see. Six months after they meet you, they won't remember your name but they **will** remember the color of the sweater you were wearing when they saw you. Then, there are the auditory people who just hear it once and can recite it word for word! I hate those people. You really have to watch what you say to them.

The toucher-smellers are a little weird because they have to **touch and smell** everything to connect to it. Don't go to a nice restaurant with one of those people. They pick up their food with their hands and sniff it before they eat it.

Which one am I? The more I think about it, I'm an auditory person. I need to hear things to validate them. The other day, I told my (girlfriend/boyfriend), "**You never tell me you love me.**" (He/She) looked at me and said, "**Are you kidding? I washed your car yesterday! Didn't I?**"

(Beat)

You see? That was a visual response. They wanted me to **see** what they did. But I wanted to **hear** something from them... not see it. I wanted to hear the word **love**. I'm a word person... and words are important to me. What they did was **show** me love. Who the hell needs that?

#30 WASH YOUR HANDS

No matter how old you are, some things just stick in your head and you never can forget them. When I was three or four years old playing in a sandbox and my mother called me in for dinner. Her voice high over my head called me out "**Time to eat! And "Wash your hands!"** She would say it deliberate and slow with each word standing out on its own instead of just saying it in a sentence.

Something like this, **"Wash... Your... Hands... "** Maybe she held out the word **hands** a little longer. And you're asking what would happen after that? Easy. I would wash my hands. You might be thinking that this was something that she only told me as a child. No way... she kept saying it to me even when I became an adult. To say the least, it stuck.

My mother passed away several years ago... but you guessed it. I can still hear her voice calling out to me from beyond. **"Wash... Your... Hands.... "** and you guessed it. I still wash them.

Thanks mom... for turning me into Howard Hughes... thanks for that compulsion I feel the moment after I shake someone's hand to immediately scrub down like a surgeon. As I scrub, I still can hear your voice... **"Wash Your Hands!"**

(Beat)

Sorry, I hope I didn't get too carried away. Did we just shake hands... you know just a moment ago... when we first met?

Gotta go... I'll be right back.

#31 ELMER FUDD PULLING THE TRAIN WHISTLE

You know the cartoon character Elmer Fudd? He was the little bald guy who chased Bugs Bunny. He usually wore a large hunting hat and shotgun… and when he spoke he had distinctive way of speaking. **"Be vewwy, vewwy quiet…I'm hunting wabbits!"** You know who I'm talking about?

(Beat)

Yeah, that's him.

Well, I had this dream the other night that I was a passenger on a super modern bullet train careening down a long track through a mountain pass. Going maybe one hundred and twenty miles an hour. Elmer Fudd was the engineer with his hunting hat on, pulling the train whistle as we rocketed over a narrow bridge, through a dark tunnel and then right over the edge… down… down… down… until we hit the bottom of a deep ravine. As we went down, Fudd grumbled **"That darwn wabbit!"** Then, the train crashed and exploded. When the smoke cleared, Elmer Fudd was totally covered in black soot with only the whites of his eyes showing. I turned to him and said, **"Eh, what's up doc?"** He looked back at me and replied, **"I hate wabbits**…" Then, the morning sun hit my eyes and I woke up.

(Beat)

I thought to myself, **"That was the strangest dream…"** As I put a carrot in the juicer for my breakfast.

#32 PAPER PLANES

When I was a kid I used to love to get old lined notebook paper and fold it into the shape of a paper plane. Sometimes I'd make a whole bunch of them and fly them around the house. Other times, I'd use them like flying spears and try to hit my dog. I'd stalk him like prey in the jungle to an imaginary water hole, and when the time was right, take my shot. If I missed, he would pick up my flying spear in his teeth and joyfully rip it apart. I guess I'd do the same, if I were him.

(Beat)

Ya'know, now that I think back on it. After a while, he would rip apart anything made of paper... and as I recall on at least one occasion... my dog really did eat my homework.

#33 LITTLE WHITE LIES

Little white lies are what you say when you don't really want to say the truth.

(Beat)

Why can't you say the truth?

You can't say the truth because you feel you should only say nice things

Or say nothing at all.

Because

That's want Thumper the rabbit said in **Bambi.**

Or because

You don't want to deal with the blowback.

Or even worse

You don't have a clue what the truth really is….

So you don't know what to say…

Like not knowing the difference between the color orange and red

Or, even worse…

Not caring enough to say anything.

#34 ELEPHANT DREAM

I think I was daydreaming when I was on the subway yesterday somewhere near Lex and 59th when all of a sudden, everything stopped and I found myself sitting in the dark. Nothing new on New York subways. But this time it felt different. It was not just dark, but that kind of blackness you feel when you're having a nightmare. There was an unsettling quiet as we all sat in total blackness… waiting. Then, for no logical reason, I found myself getting out of my seat, stepping out of the car, onto what felt like the platform and out into the blackness. But something was different. It was another place entirely. I found myself walking in Africa under a night sky where stars glittered clear like jewels. I slumbered through the dry brush of the Serengeti searching for water and my family. A soft wind gently guided me as the dry grass crackled beneath my feet. In the distance, a jackal's cry echoed through the warm summer sky. I was alone and searching for someone I knew in the vast blackness. But they were gone. I felt an emptiness I have never felt before.

(Beat)

Then, just as quickly as I got there, the car jerked forward and I was on the train again. My eyes opened, and I was back in my seat. The lights flickered, and we were on our way. The iron wheels clicked out a steady mechanical rhythm over the metal track. As they did, I closed my eyes again and as I stretched my legs out under the seat in front of me I heard the distant cry of the jackal mixing with the warm wind of the Serengeti.

#35 ROAD KILL

Don't talk to me like that. Especially after I washed your car and cleaned out all the soda cans... and candy wrappers out of the back seat. Shit, haven't you ever heard of recycling?

(Beat)

And now you're complaining because I didn't scrape the squirrel fur off your rear tire. That's going to far.

(Beat)

You were driving so damn fast that that little bastard didn't stand a chance when he ran across the double yellow lines in the road. Not a chance. Ever think that he might have had a family that was depending on him for food? Ever think of that?

(Beat)

Nah, you only think about yourself... it's always all about you... and the rest of the world for you is just... well just road kill. You just run us all over while you're on your way to wherever you're going. We're just road kill.

#36 DEFRIENDED

    O M G I can't believe you defriended me. We've been **"friends"** for at least ten months… maybe a year. I know I haven't posted much. But I did **"like"** your post about the starving puppy you found in the Bloomingdale's bag. I thought it was sweet that you adopted it… and I am really sorry you got kicked out of your apartment. I hope it wasn't the **"Puppy Balloons"** I left outside your apartment door? I mean I know a lot of people who have pets in places that say they don't allow pets. They still have them anyway… and they're fine. The **"No Pet"** rule is usually not the type of thing that you would get kicked out for… I mean I really hardly know you other than that one time we spoke in the elevator when I dropped that bag of pea soup and stained your paints. That's really how all this got started. I looked you up. It was that simple. Remember? And now… without warning you defriended me! O M G I can't believe you would do that after all we've been through.

    L O L

#37 IF YOU WALK AWAY

Look we're having a fight. That's all it is. Nothing more. We both said a few things just now that we will be sorry we said when the morning comes. But leaving? What's that?

You stay and fight! You say what you say and I say what I say and that's it.

So, step away from that door. If you walk away now… if you leave this room, it will be over forever. There will be nothing and I mean nothing to say in the morning

#38 HAPPY FOR YOU

I'm so happy for you! Congratulations! It couldn't have happened to a better person. You worked hard and really had it coming to you.

(Beat)

All of it. Okay, I have to admit I'm a little jealous. Just a little. But nothing I can't handle.

(Beat)

Well okay, I'm a little miffed. I guess some people have all the luck and then there's the rest of us… who can't get a damn break if their life depended on it. That's me… I'm always at the **right place** at the **wrong time**… or even worse…. the **wrong place** at the **wrong time**. It really really sucks to be me!

(Beat)

But… I'm so so happy for you!

#39 TEXTING

Where are you now?

In my car

Cool – what are you doing?

Driving. Doing my nails.

Where?

Freeway… so much traffic… stop and go… stop and go.

Where you going?

Class. I have a test I'm late. Unhappy face

U studying?

Studying now…

Cool

(Beat)

Cool.

What are you gonna do later?

Nothing

Cool.

Wanna hang out?

Excellent.

Your place?

Cool.

#40 THE ESSAY

I'm sitting here trying to come up with at least five characteristics of the Renaissance and my mind is a blank page. I was prepared to take this test. It's all up here. (Point to head)

(Beat)

Problem is gotta get it down here on the page. And really, there's a big space between what's up here and what I need to put down there. I mean I knew it in the car on the way over here. But now, when I have to put the actual words down on paper… nothing comes out?

That's why I hate essay tests. I'm a **"True and False"** person… all the way. No jerking around. It's either you're right or you're wrong. You at least get a fifty fifty shot at it. But this essay crap requires you to think…. I hate that.

(Beat)

Now, if I can just think of a nifty way to write the first line, maybe it will all come back to me.

#41 THE TIARA (Male)

It was this chick's birthday and she showed up at school wearing a crown on her head. I said to her, **"What's with the crown?"** She turned wicked and snapped at me, "**It's a tiara! You idiot!**" Wow… that was harsh. It seemed like such an intense reaction to what I said. Then, she smiled and adjusted her **"tiara"** on her head to make sure it was just right and walked off.

(Beat)

Whatever? It's still a crown to me and really… she's the one that's the idiot if she thinks anyone gives a crap that it's her birthday. Wearing a tiara is not going to change that!

#42 THE BABY BENCH

It's funny the crap you think about from when you were a kid. Okay, this is going to sound weird. When I was in kindergarten, my classroom had a wooden bench in the corner of the room that my teacher called the "Baby Bench." If you were not good, you would be forced to sit on the "Baby Bench" and suffer the humiliation of being one that was not mature enough to be with the rest of the students. Ergo, you were reduced to being a **little baby** and suffer the ridicule of your fellow classmates. You didn't have to do much to land in the "Baby Bench." If you were caught talking, being awake during naptime or just normally horsing around, you could find yourself sitting on the "Baby Bench."

(Beat)

As an adult, I can look back on all that and proudly say that I never once got the "Baby Bench." Not once! Well almost once, when I dipped one of Susan Happy's pigtails in a jar of red poster paint. She screamed bloody murder and I almost got caught. But, I lucked out because my teacher didn't actually see me do it. It was a bonehead move... but sometimes you gotta do what you gotta do, no matter what the price. Like parking in a red zone when you're in a hurry... I wonder if they have a "Baby bench" for that?

#43 CONTEMPLATION OF SELF

You ever feel that no matter **what** you do it's never enough? That you never quite achieve the intended goal that you set out for? It can be anything big or small. Going on a diet, working out at the gym, making more money… or it could be a very slight insignificant goal such as making a list of things to do and checking each one off as you do it. There comes the rub. What if you make a list of five things and only do four? As you do each one, you get an uncomfortable feeling within yourself that is so disturbing that you're not going to make it to the end of the list. At the end of the day, you've done four out of the five things you have set out to do… but what do you do? Instead of celebrating what you have accomplished you focus on that one incomplete item. This unsettling feeling keeps growing and becomes an affront to the very thing you are attempting. You try to cope with these never-ending pangs of insecurity by spending every waking moment of your life in contemplation of your self-condition. You are literally consumed with an aura of your own self-loathing.

(Beat, take a breath)

It's an endless spiral with only momentary snippets of sunlight coming through the clouds when you sigh and say to yourself. **"Ya'know my life is pretty damn good right now and I'm actually happy."**

The morning sun warms your face and for that brief moment, and you find comfort. But only for a moment… then it starts all over again.

#44 TUESDAY

Out of all the days of the week the one I hate the most is Tuesday. Monday sucks too because it's back to work and all that crap. But Tuesday... reaffirms it to be true and says to me, "**If you thought Monday sucked, now it's Tuesday... and it's not any better is it? And you still have the rest of the week ahead of you.**"

Wednesday is **"hump day."** Thursday is the day, I think will never end and Friday... well by then I'm so damn tired and bored that I don't care about anything except quitting time.

(Beat)

Now Saturday, I know I should like that day. It should be a **"no pressure day."** Just hanging out and just letting it flow. I like that idea of that day. But Saturday sucks too. Why? Because it's "do all the chores that you don't have time for during the week day." So I spend my Saturdays, doing mundane crap like laundry and cleaning the house. So what's left, Sunday? And what do I do on Sunday when I am so tired and spent? Just one thing... **"sleep"**

(Beat)

Now that, I like a lot.

#45 MICKEY MOUSE T-SHIRT

Okay, here's a question, **"Do you think it's a cool thing for a guy to wear a Mickey Mouse T-shirt?"** You know the one with Mickey's smiling face and his ears sticking out from side to side. I was thinking that his ears come out to the right and left at just about where your breast nipples are under your shirt. So do you think, it's okay for a guy to wear one of those or do you think it takes you to a place you don't want to be… let's call it the happiest place on earth. And "happy" I mean too "happy" can't be good. I think people like you better if you're miserable or at least a little miserable. You don't want your friends thinking you're too happy. It will just create lots of uncomfortable moments that you won't want to find yourself in. So, if you ask me… I'd keep that Mickey Mouse T-shirt in the dresser drawer at least for now or at least until you feel an overwhelming sense of joy.

(Beat)

And there's absolutely nothing wrong with that!

#46 ELEMENTS OF STYLE

I have two very good friends that are interior designers. They can make almost any room of a house look like it should be in a magazine layout. I don't know how they do it? I mean how can you look at a room that's empty and know what to put in it? Or how can you see something that's incredibly ugly and make it look beautiful? I just can't do that.

(Beat)

I know what I like when I see it all done. But, I don't have the ability to see something that's not in front of me. I'm a literal thinker... when I look at something I am only able to see what it is... not what it can be. To be able to see the potential in everything and be able to present it with a certain element of style must be a real gift. I wonder if my friends have the same ability when they meet new people? To be able to see in them ... their true potential... now that would be a real talent.

#47 DREAMING OF PARIS

Going to work… the same as every other morning. The train rolls into Penn Station. I walk up the stairs from the platform toward the street level. The air is filled with the smell of urine and stale cigarettes. As I go up the escalator I diesel smoke, grease, brewing coffee and donuts. I've made it to the street and head to my office. I stay there all day until it's time to leave.

On my way home, I do the same thing… only in reverse. I ask myself what I did today but I have already forgotten. Now I approach the stairs to the platform and take one last look up at the sky before I descend. But there is no sky. It has all turned to darkness. I think to myself that I am wrapped in darkness. It is dark when I wake in the morning and dark when I go back home. At the platform, the ground shakes when my train arrives. I wonder how the double doors come to a stop at almost the same spot every night. I make my way into the car, and tonight I'm lucky… I find a seat. The train jolts forward and my long journey home has begun.

As I sit, in my seat, I see the same people I see every day wearing the same coats and hats, smelling like stale perfume and mothballs. One man pretends to fall asleep on the shoulder of a woman sitting next to him. She tries to lean away, but there is no room. Just to the left of them I see a young girl wearing a red white and blue sweatshirt, with writing on it, **"Dream of Paris."** I smile at her and sigh, **"If I only could."** She smiles back at me as the clicking rhythm of the train on the track lulls me to a soft sleep. **"If I only could."**

#48 ROMANTIC

Okay, breaking up sucks! But I am really pissed right now. You know what she said to me? (In her voice) ***"Jeffery, you're just not romantic!"***

Romantic? What's that supposed to mean anyway? So, I asked her, ***"Romantic?***

Of course I'm Romantic… what should I be doing that I'm not doing that's romantic?"

She looked at me then without a beat… started to cry. Through her tears I could hear her say, (in her voice) ***"Long walks on the beach… when it's raining…***

watching Twilight movies while we eat popcorn… and holding me close when I'm scared… and lastly… warm pizza on a Sunday afternoon.

(Beat)

Now I don't know about you, but "pizza…"

I could do that.

#49 LITTLE BLACK DRESS

Can we speak frankly? Okay, I normally don't do something like this. But... I was just sitting over there on the other side of the bar when I saw you sitting here. All alone, sipping your drink, wearing your little black dress which (by the way) looks very nice on you. I just had to leave where I was sitting and come all the way over here.

(Beat)

I was thinking to myself, *"**Georgie** (that's my name), what kind of person wears such a nice little black dress with a bow on the shoulder? Just sitting here alone? Why?"*

(Beat, no answer)

"All alone, sipping a drink with no smile."

(Beat, no answer)

Still no smile? **Now** I'm thinking to myself... maybe this person wants to be alone? **Maybe** this person is wearing this little black dress for a reason? Something sad? Maybe because someone has died?

(Beat, he takes a long look into her eyes)

"I'm so sorry. So very sorry."

#50 HEMLOCK

I never thought a day would come when I would wake up one morning and you wouldn't be there beside me. I loved the way we would have coffee and read the morning paper together. Now, when I wake up, the space where you slept, where your body once was… is just an empty impression on the bed. There is so much we could have said… but didn't… and there were so many things we said we would do **tomorrow**…. And tomorrow did come… but not the way we thought it would. We always thought that our life would stay way it was… and there would be time to do the things we dreamed of doing together.

(Beat)

And you know… we really did so many things together. The truth is, I liked you a lot and you would have certainly been my friend if you weren't my (husband/wife). In fact, you would have been my **best** friend. And now that I say it aloud, I realize that you were my best friend. Always there…

(Beat)

I miss you so much… more that you could ever know… and I wish I were with you now just like before. I would give anything for that. Anything. Anything.

(Beat)

Please don't think ill of me… but my thoughts have become darker. Just one ounce of hemlock can take me from here… to where you are.

So I can be with you again.

#51 THINGS PEOPLE SAY

I had this thought the other day while I was walking my dog. You want to know what it was?

Okay.

I was thinking that I spend a disproportionate amount of my life... my day... worrying about what other people think about me. Do they like me? What do they think about how I look? Do they really want to be around me?

Then, I thought... the truth is...

Most people don't think about me at all. They don't really care what I say, what I do or what clothes I wear. Why? They are too busy thinking about themselves. I know it probably hurts for you to hear this... but the real truth is nobody cares....

Well, they may pretend to care... but the truth is they don't. And if they do say something about you... they're really saying something about themselves.

You look fabulous! I love the color red... it's my favorite

Love those shoes! I have a pair just like them!

You're so smart... I can't believe it! No one can understand you but me!

Next time you worry about things people say... listen carefully to the words they use... you'll see, it's not about you at all... it's all about them. Once you get that, you'll be a lot happier.

#52 STATE OF GRACE

I find myself in a state of sanctification that I have never felt before. I mean I can't ever recall feeling so good about myself... the way I look, the way my body feels and the way everything seems to be going my way. I'm finally getting it.

(Beat)

Now I now what you're thinking... **"What goes up must come down.... Right?"** But you're off the mark here... this place I'm in right now... it going to be permanent. I can feel it in every fiber of my body and soul. There's no going back for me... ever... and it all has to do with you. Ever since I met you... it's all fallen into place. Everything is different. It's all good.... I feel like I can dance under a starlit sky like Fred Astaire... and you're my Ginger Rogers... gliding across the floor, without a hitch.

Together... forever.

#53 DUMB WAYS TO DIE

Dumb ways to die.

Eating a rusty nail.

Jumping out of a plane... without a parachute.

Kissing a cobra... right on the lips... and slipping your tongue in its mouth.

Sticking a fork... repeatedly... in a plugged in toaster.

Watching Twilight movies... and eating microwave popcorn... for 24 hours straight.

Walking... in Central Park... at three in the morning... singing "I'm in the money."

Brushing your teeth... with super glue.

Sitting in a crowded jail cell... humming... "I'm in the Mood for Love."

Wearing a Star Trek costume at a Star Wars convention.

Dating someone... anyone... that's a serial killer. Then trying to break up with them.

Sticking a #2 pencil up a polar bear's ass... and waiting.

Sneezing so hard while eating spaghetti... that the noodles come out your nose.

Hiding a tarantula in your underwear... while going through an airport pat down.

Using a chain saw... to give yourself an eyebrow trim... in the dark.

Going up to a bank teller... wearing a bag over your head... singing the Ludacris rap song... "Stick em Up bitch! Stick em up!"

(Music plays – Ludacris's Stick Em Up)

(Exit)

#54 I ALWAYS REMIND PEOPLE OF OTHER PEOPLE

You ever meet someone and they instantly tell you that you remind them of someone else that they used to know? No? Well it happens to me all the time. When I meet them, it starts off fine for the first minute or so and then WAM! It happens and they say something like:

"I can't believe this, you so remind me of..." (You can insert someone's name here) or they might say **"you are so much like"** (insert someone's name there) and then they pick one of my body parts. They'll say: **"It's your mouth, or your, hair... your shirt that reminds me so much of..."** (Insert someone's name here). It doesn't really matter what they say, because after that moment, to them you are no longer you. You are the "other" person they know and with that comes a certain expectation that you do everything just like the person that you remind them of does. You are expected to be that person or they will end the conversation.

(Beat)

I mean why can't they just like me for me? Why do I have to be (insert someone's name here)? Am I not my own person or just a carbon copy of someone I don't even know? Why can't I just be me? Isn't that enough?

(Exit)

#55 AT LEAST YOU'RE NOT LYING

Now just relax. Don't move and most importantly don't try to say anything. I wouldn't be able to understand you anyway with your hands tied like that and that gag in your mouth. First of all, I'm not going to hurt you. I promise that there is no physical harm intended here… I just want to talk to you. Get something off my chest and I don't want to be interrupted.

(Beat)

So, if you're quiet… we can't this done right away. Okay? Good. Where do I start? Okay. I mean I could make this a **long** story… but I won't. I mean you probably have places to go… people to see. I know I do. Okay, here goes. You have led me on and allowed me to falsely believe that there was something special between us. You have lied to me… haven't you? You have lied to the point of making a total fool of me. It's bad enough that you're married and never bothered to tell me. And why would you tell me that you loved me when you didn't mean it? Why? Oh no… please don't try to say anything… it would only be more lies wrapped up in yet more lies… No, don't try and talk… at least when you're **not** talking…. you're not lying. Right? To you a lie is just words you use to get what you want. But I believe that words actually matter. (Beat, pulls out a knife or other pointed object)

Don't worry about this knife. ***I'm not going to use it on you.***

Actually, that was just a lie… I just told you a lie. See? I can lie too… and well now, you're going to find out what it feels like.

#56 EXHALE

Of course I like you. Why wouldn't you ever think that I **didn't** like you? If I seemed put off it's because I was surprised that you knew so much about me. You have to admit that we've only briefly spoken maybe two or three times. So, when you blurted out my date of birth, the names of all my pets (past and present) and then rattled off by heart every place that I have ever lived in, I was **"put back."** No, I was amazed that that sort of information is out there and you were able to get it. Then when you recited the name of every teacher I have ever had going back to kindergarten, I was… what can I say **speechless.** I am totally in awe of your ability to garner such intimate… no such detailed information about me. I would imagine that all of this is out there… somewhere on the Internet or the cloud if you know where to look for it. And obviously you **know** where to look for it.

(Beat)

Of course I like you. Really I can't say much more because I am at a disadvantage. You seem to know so much about me but I, on the other hand, know so little… about you. When I asked your name, I wasn't being rude… I truly wanted to know. And when you told me that your name was exactly the same as mine… I was **silent.** Yes, it's true. But that's because I was, what can I say… breathless… and was left with nothing else to say… except to perhaps… exhale.

#57 NOCTURNE

Sometimes at night when the full moon covets the warmth of passing clouds and its glow softens the night sky, I dream of you. You stand before me, white and silken with the light of heaven above you. And you smile and reach toward me. Our hands touch and then we are drawn closer together, softly until my chest gently touches your breast and I can feel your heart beating against mine. Our eyes touch upon our souls and we are one. The night is ours for the keeping. I whisper gently "**I love you more than life itself** " as we dance under the night sky until morning light

#58 LIKE BUTTER

    Listen up. You just knock on the door three times. Like this… knock, knock, knock. When they look through the peephole and ask who sent you… you tell' em… Jilly sent you. They'll ask: **Who's your favorite cartoon character?**" You say: "**Felix the Cat…**" That's it. After that… all you gotta do is walk in. When you get inside, don't get all stiff and nervous; just pick up the envelope at the bar. They'll know what to do.

    Go up to the bar and the bar keep will give you a small paper envelope. If it's *green*, you take the envelope and you put it in your right jacket pocket. If it's *blue*, you take the envelope and put it in your left jacket pocket. You got that? Good.

    Then, they'll ask you if you want a drink… and you shake your head "No." Don't say "No" just shake your head "No." Then, turn around and walk outta there. Don't walk too fast and don't walk too slow. Okay, you got it?

    Sure thing… nice and easy… just like butter.

#59 GOING HOME

It's about ten after six... I'm so tired I don't even know if I can pick myself out of my chair. My eyes can only see blurred lines on my computer screen in the half-light coming through small window behind me. Outside on the street below, the dim glow of traffic lights makes a red line against the orange sky and the setting sun. My computer slowly grinds its way to off as I clear away a stack of papers that have been in front of me all day. I put them in two piles – "tomorrow" and "today." I slide "tomorrow" to my left and "today" to my right creating a narrow open space in the center on my desktop. My back strains as I slowly get up from my chair. I step on a bent paperclip that has been on the floor next to my foot all day. I let is stay there as I put on my jacket and slowly close the door behind me. I won't have to turn the lights off as I leave. That happens automatically.

I'm going home.

#60 PLEASE DON'T TRY THIS AT HOME

Putting your socks in the garbage disposal… while it's running.

Chopping onions with a hatchet… in the dark

Playing with a baby's rattler… in front of a rattlesnake.

Watching "Singing in the Rain"… in the shower

Giving your cat a bath… then drying it in the clothes dryer

Cutting a hole in your roof to see the sky… on a rainy day

Walking… on the ceiling.

Feeding an elephant in your living room… and not taking it for a walk afterwards.

Phoning random people you don't know… and inviting them over at midnight.

Writing your name a hundred times… on your living room wall… with black marker.

Inventing something worth millions of dollars then forgetting what it was.

Putting a whole bunch of junk in a box… then burying it in a deep hole… with cement… and then not being able to find your car keys.

(Shrug shoulders and exit)

#61 COOKING A POUND CAKE

I wish I could create the perfect mate. Someone I could fall in love with and be with the rest of my life. Let me tell you. I've been looking for a long time and there's just isn't anyone out there. I know what you're going to say. We live in an imperfect world and love is really about compromise.

(Beat)

Screw compromise. I want the perfect mate and I can visualize them right here and now just like I would if I gave you a recipe for a pound cake. Why pound cake? Because it's simple, to the point and goes with everything.

Lot's of butter and vegetable shortening

Plenty of sugar. Some eggs and flour

A little bit of salt, baking powder and

Let's not forget the vanilla extract.

Not too fancy but still elegant. Beautiful, and yummy, pound cake… that always brings a smile to your face. Yep, falling in love is like cooking a pound cake.

Really.

Think about it.

#62 A TEMPORARY PET

I've been going out with (Fred/Sheila) for about a month now. And it's been great. Well, really not **"great."** More like **"okay."** You know how it goes. It all starts out really wonderful and ever so slowly it goes from there to just **"okay."** It's not like there's one big thing that I can say really bothers me. It's lots of little things that add up. Okay, here's a for instance. When we go out to dinner, (he/she) always comments on my order. **"You're going to eat meat? I can't believe you would eat a cow? Don't you like cows?"** Then there was the other night at the movies when (he/she) had to hold the bucket of popcorn. I felt like I had to ask permission each time I put my hand in the bucket. And really, what's with the constant use of hand sanitizer every time we go through a doorway. I hate the smell of that stuff. Last night some of it got on my hair… don't ask me how.

(Beat)

So, yes, life goes on and I'm not going to stress about this… but really, as soon as someone **"better"** comes a long… (Fred/Sheila) is history. What can I say?

(He/She) is just… a temporary pet.

#63 NECKTIE PARLOR

When I walked in the lights were pretty low so I didn't notice it at first... then it hit me as I looked all around the room. Everyone was wearing a necktie. Let me clarify... not the women just the guys. I knew this was a really nice restaurant but I had no idea that there was a dress code. I mean, who wears ties anymore? Nobody.

I never wear a tie to the office... that's because I don't work in an office. I'm a writer and my office is anywhere I choose it to be. It's not that I'm **anti tie**. If someone wants to wear a tie, that's their prerogative. I'm good with that and it should end right there.

(Beat)

Look at the way they're all looking at me. I am dressed pretty nice. I'm not some slob off the street. I think I paid $80 for this shirt and my jacket... it's a few years old so I'm not really sure. But it must have been at least two or three hundred bucks. My jeans were $200 on sale and my boots... leather and very expensive. Shit, I've probably got over a thousand dollars on me right now!

(Beat)

The maître di is showing me to my table. So, I think I'm okay. Not going to stress. I'm just gonna walk right in and sit down at my table and enjoy dinner. Yeah, my table, right over here... in the back... by the kitchen door.

#64 MELANCHOLY

    I hate it when you leave. I have no reason to feel this way but I just do. It starts when you get out of bed. I know it's coming. You look into the bathroom mirror then turn on the shower. This is my signal to get up too because I know you'll be gone soon. I wait for you outside the shower door. After your shower, you get dressed. The part I hate the most is when I hear the sound of your shoes dropping on the floor. They have no laces and you slip them on one at a time. That tells me that you will leave me very soon. Shortly after that you fill my water bowl with fresh water. Then, you feed me. You gently put the bright blue ceramic bowl down and pat me on the head. I pretend to be excited about the chicken and kibble you've given me, but I really hate it. A minute after that, your coat is on and you tip toe quietly out the door. You try not to close the door hard as you leave as if I didn't know what you were doing. After you're gone, a strange silence overcomes the house that consumes me. I know I can go out the small door into the yard but it doesn't help because you're not there. There is nothing I can do but remain in this void and wait… until you return.

65 THIS TIME

I climb the long stairway up to her place as I have done at least a thousand times before. But today, something is different. I don't know what? Maybe it's the way the light hits the stairway when I open the front door. As I slowly climb to the top of the stairway, I notice the shattered sticks of what was a chair the night before. I smashed it into her wall. Now, the sticks are neatly tied together with a piece of rope and look more like a pile of wood than a chair. When I reach the top of the stairs, she hears me coming and calls out my name. Her voice sounds friendly and warm and you would have never known that we fought so violently the night before. She calls out my name again and I am about to answer her but I don't. Something inside of me just can't do it... this time.

(Beat)

I stand silently frozen in the moment at the top of the stairs and before I know it, I'm walking back down toward the front door. I just can't do it anymore and I need to leave. I know I have left before... and then have come back again. But this time... it feels different.

She calls out my name one more time as I get to the bottom of the stairs I open the front door and walk toward the street. The fresh air feels good on my face. I'm not sure if I will come back again. I might but this time, I just keep walking away toward the street and the morning light.

#66 DECONSTRUCTION

Okay, I'm not in a relationship right now. Happy? I know how much we all value the interplay between human beings, but sometimes you just have to be alone. You know what I mean? Look I've tried the whole relationship thing and in the beginning everything is all hot and heavy… and new. You think to yourself, this person is nice. I like being with them and when we're together we have a great time. But then it hits maybe about a week or two into it. They start taking you apart piece by piece so they can make you in their own image. I mean haven't they ever heard of opposites attract? I guess not. They start taking you apart changing everything that makes **"you"** you! The clothes you wear, the food you eat, what you like, what you dislike… they keep digging until they reach your very soul. When they change that… you no longer exist. You've become… someone else. They have remade you in their own image. They look at you and see themselves. Sounds Biblical right? But, you know what happens after that? They get board with you because, after all, you have become them and they're no longer interested in you. They have destroyed the very reason they were attracted to you in the first place. Then what happens?

(Beat)

You break up! And you're alone again. Like I am now. Happy?

(Exit)

#67 ALWAYS

I can't believe you still look the same as the last time I saw you. How many years has it been? At least thirty years. It's been a lifetime and we have lived out most of our lives with more yesterdays behind us than tomorrows to come. But for me, you are just like the last day I saw you. It was at our high school graduation day. It was June and it was hotter than hell. You looked so cute in your cap and gown. You probably don't, but I remember that day actually very well. I walked toward you. I think you were with your family. Mom and dad… brothers. There was something I wanted to say to you. That's why I tapped you gently on your shoulder. You quickly turned and smiled at me. That made me feel really good… and then you stuck out your hand and said: **"Good luck in your future endeavors. "** I think I said thanks, and was about to say what I came to say, but you turned around and went right back into your conversation. We never spoke again… until today. And you know what? I still want to tell it to you. No please don't turn away. I have got to say this.

(Beat)

I have always loved you, probably starting in sixth grade all through high school. I loved you more than anything else in my life and I probably still do now. I have never forgotten you… you have been there… **always…** and always will.

You don't have to say anything back to me. Not a word.

I just wanted to say it to you. Let you know… how I felt.

#68 IF I COULD ONLY BE THIN

You ever notice that thin people always get everything they want? Life seems to always go their way? Think about it. All the movie stars, rock musicians like Mick Jagger… and what about all those fashion models? Thin! I guess the way the universe works is… the thinner you are the more you get. You ever see a chubby person get a break? No way… it's the back of the line for them. They are destined to live mediocre lives at best.

(Beat)

Now take me… I'm hardly overweight. But, let's face it I'm not thin. I'm in the **"normal"** slightly chunky category. And really, I don't eat that much. It's just everything I eat goes directly to my stomach and ass. Just look at me. What do you think? How do I look? You think I look fine? Why am I not surprised? That's what everyone says. But let me ask you this. Would you like me better if I were thinner?

(Beat)

I knew it! How about **really** thin? Look I'll bite on my cheeks, pull in my stomach and stand on my toes. Now, what do you think? Do you like me more? Well… well? Hello? Where did you go? Shit.

(Bites cheeks, sucks in stomach, tip toes and exits.)

#69 SHAMAN

(Whisper like chant)

Horeesha... Horeesha... Great hawk of the sky, I call upon you now to come among us. Here before me is a mortal with a heart of peace who is in need. Ha na Horeesha... Great hawk of the sky... God of creation who brought us life from the primordial sea... come among us now. Horeesha... Horeesha...Horeesha....

(A large inhale, stillness, then a deep voice speaks.)

Mortal stand before me... I feel a restless soul... longing for the quiet of morning... you have been that way since the day you were born. But your spirit cannot find peace because you are haunted by the spirits of your people... they are all gone now and you are the last one... they call upon you for justice! It is born by a mark you bare since birth... a mark that is unmistakable... under your left arm. It is there because the spirits tell me so... The mark, of the trinity... of water, earth and fire. You are the last of your people... The Fire... and through you... they will rise again. Like the eternal flame they will rise again...

(Large exhale as the spirit leaves his body. He speaks again as himself.)

The great spirit has left us. I must rest.

(His eyes close as a peaceful stillness surrounds him)

#70 CRACKIN ROCKS

    I hate my job... okay, now it's out in the open. I really hate my job... and **everything** about it. I go into work every morning, sit in the same chair, in the same cubical, see the same people in the same stale fluorescent light. I sit in front of my computer screen and enter data from one pile of papers, into the little boxes on the screen so I can print them out and place them into another pile of paper on the other side of my desk. Above it all the soft rock station plays the same music and the same commercials it did the day before. The one thing that's certain is that nothing changes. It's the same everyday. I take a ten-minute break around nine-thirty, get a cup of burnt coffee and a granola bar that's hard as a rock. At ten minutes to noon, I get up, go to the restroom and wash up for lunch. I go to lunch where I order the same turkey cheese sandwich and diet coke that I had the day before. Sometime after one o'clock I'm back in front of the computer screen. But for some reason, I'm very tired. I fight to keep my eyes open and do the best I can to get to three o'clock. That's when I get a second cup of burnt coffee and another granola bar. Then, it's back to the computer screen and I push as hard as I can until ten minutes to five. Then I stop.

    (Beat)

    That's my job. It's just like one of those old black and white prison movies. There's a line of prisoners dressed in striped suits each with a black ball chained to their feet. Standing in a line... under the hot sun... pounding sledgehammers in unison from dawn till dusk. Not making anything special. Just "**crackin rocks.**"

Printed in Great Britain
by Amazon